101 VACATION JOKES

by Jovial Bob Stine

Illustrated by Rick Mujica

SCHOLASTIC INC.
New York Toronto London Auckland Sydney

FOR MATTY
With thanks for the jokes!

ISBN 0-590-43610-4

Text copyright © 1990 by R.L. Stine. Illustrations copyright © 1990 by Scholastic Inc. All rights reserved. Published by Scholastic Inc.

21 20   9/9 0 1 2/0

Printed in the U.S.A.   01

First Scholastic printing, May 1990

DON'T LEAVE HOME
WITHOUT THESE JOKES!

What is the pig's favorite vacation
spot?

Wallow Wallow, Washington.

Why did the leopard have a lousy
vacation?

He couldn't find the right spot.

Why did the elephant have a lousy
vacation?

The airline lost his trunk!

What do you call a very young dog
that travels around the world?

A puppy.

What do you call a mouse that visits
a lion on his vacation?

Dinner.

Where do ducks go on their vacation?

Albe-quacky, New Mexico!

Where did the chicken go on her vacation?

To Fowl-adelphia.

Where did the other chicken go on her vacation?

To Sandy Eggo.

WHO HAD A GOOD VACATION?

Did the shark have a good vacation?

Yes, it was very en-jaw-able!

Did the owl have a good vacation?

Yes, it was a hoot!

Did the pig have a good vacation?

Yes, it was swill.

Did the chicken have a good vacation?

No, it laid an egg!

Did the skunk have a good vacation?

No, it stunk!

Did the dalmation have a good
vacation?

In spots.

Did the cat have a good vacation?

Yes, it was purr-fect.

Did the mummy have a good vacation?

Who knows? He was too wrapped up to tell us!

Did the cow have a good vacation?

No, it was an udder disaster!

vacation?

Did the hyena have a good vacation?

Yes, it was a lot of laughs!

Did the pelican have a good vacation?

No, the bill was too big!

VACATION VUNNYSTUFF

Tim: You slept under the car during your vacation?! Why?

Jim: I wanted to get up oily in the morning!

Max: What's the weather like?

Pam: I don't know. It's too cloudy to see!

Henry: You can't decide where to go on your vacation? Do you always have trouble making decisions?
Larry: Yes and no.

Kim: Welcome back from vacation. How'd you get the bad gash on your forehead?
Tim: I bit myself.
Kim: Don't be ridiculous. How could you bite yourself on the forehead?
Tim: I stood on a chair!

Vacationer: We're in Cabin Three. Does the rain always come through the roof like this?

Owner: No, sir. Only when it rains!

Bus Passenger: Hi! I'm vacationing in your town. Does this bus stop at Elm Street?

2nd Passenger: Yes, it does. Just watch me, and get off one stop before I do.

Policeman: You're not allowed to fish here.

Max: I'm not fishing. I'm giving my pet worm a bath!

Josh: Do you know why the Statue of Liberty stands in New York harbor?

Jim: Because it can't sit down??

Mike: We lost our dog while we were on vacation.

Mark: Why not put an ad in the newspaper "Lost & Found" column?

Mike: Don't be ridiculous. He can't read!

Nick and Mick were arranging to meet on vacation. "If I get there first," said Nick, "I'll mark a chalk line on the wall."

"Good idea," said Mick. "And if I get there first, I'll rub it off!"

Mark and Mike went fishing on their vacation and trespassed onto a private lake. The town policeman came by and spotted them. "Hey, didn't you see that sign?" he asked.

"Sure," said Mark. "But it said 'Private' at the top, so I didn't read the rest!"

Sally: We went to France on our vacation. I'm so glad I wasn't born there.

Susie: Why?

Sally: I can't speak French!

Mike: I went to Switzerland on my vacation.

Mick: Really? What did you think of the scenery?

Mike: Oh, I couldn't see much. There were all those mountains in the way!

Pam: Uh oh. I just swallowed a roll of film!

Doctor: Don't worry. Nothing serious can develop!

Susie and Sally went to the circus on their vacation. "I thought the knife-thrower was terrible!" exclaimed Susie.

"Why?" Sally asked.

"Well, he threw all those knives at that girl and didn't hit her once!"

TAKE THESE JOKES ANYWHERE!

Where did Sylvester Stallone go on his vacation?

To the Rocky Mountains.

Where did the doctor go on her vacation?

To Ill-inois.

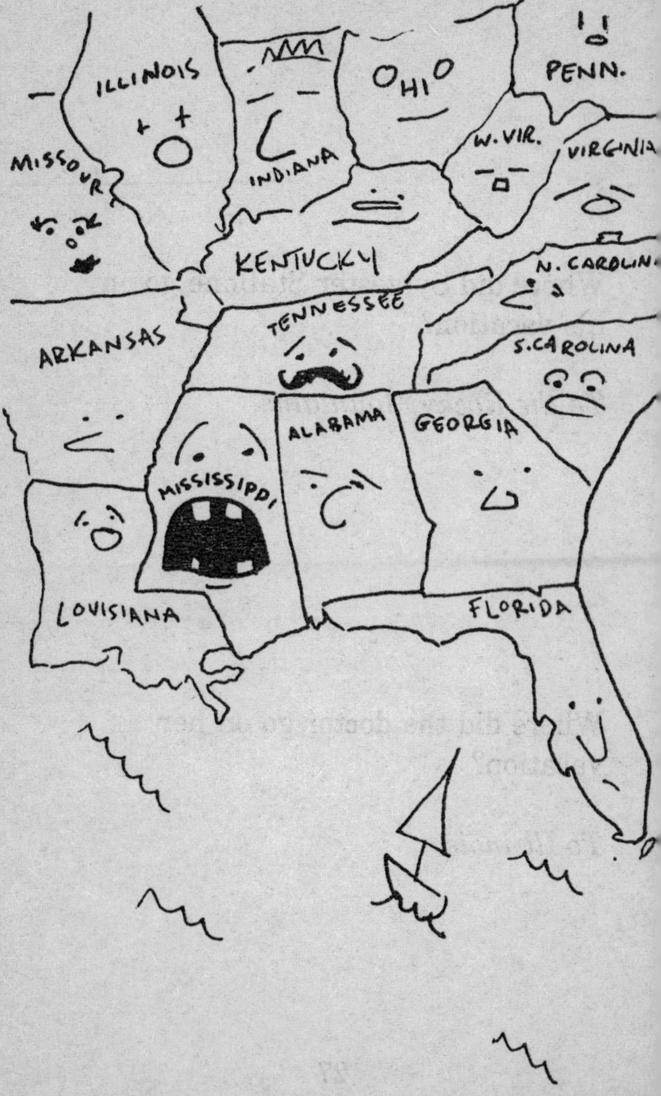

ILLINOIS
INDIANA
OHIO
PENN.
MISSOURI
W. VIR.
VIRGINIA
KENTUCKY
N. CAROLINA
TENNESSEE
ARKANSAS
S. CAROLINA
ALABAMA
GEORGIA
MISSISSIPPI
LOUISIANA
FLORIDA

Where did the dentist go on his
vacation?

To the mouth of the Mississippi.

Where did the plumber go on his vacation?

To Flushing, New York.

Where did Santa Claus go on his vacation?

To a ho-ho-ho-tel.

Where did the fortune-teller go on her vacation?

To Palm Beach.

Where did Tarzan go on his vacation?

To Hollywood & Vine.

Where did the hatmaker go on her vacation?

To the Kentucky Derby.

Where did the jockey go on his vacation?

To Gallup, New Mexico.

Where did the wave go on her vacation?

To the shore.

Where did the candymaker go on his vacation?

First to Carmel, California, then to the Mint.

VACATION PREDICTIONS!

There will be 56 straight days of sunshine, not a single drop of rain — until the morning you and your family leave for your vacation!

PREDICTIONS:

At least one of your friends will report seeing a shark — even though they are vacationing in Ohio!

When it's sunny, at least 700 people will say, "Hot enough for you?" When it's cloudy, at least 700 people will say, "Be careful. You know you get the worst sunburn when it's overcast!"

Even though you coat yourself with insect repellent, mosquitoes will ignore everyone else in the state and demonstrate a strange attraction to you!

You will work 20 minutes and sprain both wrists and your back trying to get into a wet bathing suit!

PREDICTION:

No one will be watching when you do a perfect reverse double somersault dive from the high board. Everyone will be watching when you belly flop into the water, splashing a group of old ladies and little children.

PREDICTION:

You will give yourself third-degree burns by sitting down on your car's plastic seat covers after the car has been in the sun for eight hours!

PREDICTIONS:

Your three new summer allergies will be ice cream, swimming-pool water, and fresh air!

All of your friends who are going away will promise to write. But the only mail you'll get will be an overdue book notice from the library.

The lifeguard at the pool, who you think is smiling at you, is actually laughing at your attempts to do the butterfly!

You will lighten your hair to blond and tell everyone the sun did it!

PREDICTION:
You'll get mosquito bites only in places where it's impossible to scratch!

DON'T KNOCK THESE
VACATION KNOCK-KNOCKS

Knock-knock.
Who's there?
Al.
Al who?
Al be back from vacation in two
   weeks!

Knock-knock.
Who's there?
Carl.
Carl who?
Carl me a taxi. I want to go to the
  airport.

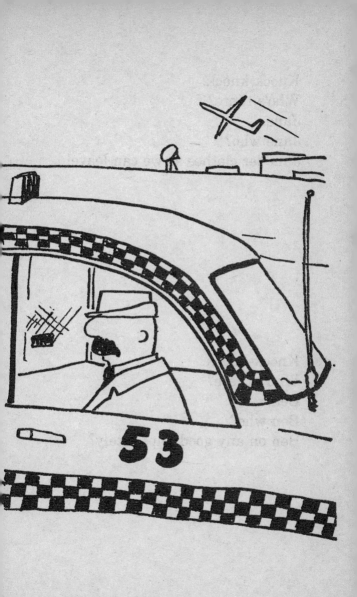

53

Knock-knock.
Who's there?
Jane.
Jane who?
Jane jer clothes so we can leave!

Knock-knock.
Who's there?
Ben.
Ben who?
Ben on any good trips lately?

Knock-knock.
Who's there?
Fred.
Fred who?
Fred you have to read more of these
vacation knock-knocks before the
book is finished!

Knock-knock.
Who's there?
Wayne.
Wayne who?
Wayne, Wayne, go away. I want only
sunny days on my vacation!

Knock-knock.
Who's there?
Me.
Me who?
I've been on vacation only two days
and you don't remember me??

WHAT DID THEY DO?

What did the eye doctor do on her vacation?

She made a spectacle of herself!

What did the trapeze artist do on his vacation?

He really let go!

What did the accordion-player do on his vacation?

He got into a tight squeeze!

What did the clockmaker do on her vacation?

She learned how to unwind!

What did the bulldozer driver do on his vacation?

He just dozed off!

Why did the gymnast enjoy her vacation?

She bent over backward to have a good time!

Did the janitor have a good time at the Las Vegas casino?

Yes, he cleaned up!

MORE VACATION VUNNYSTUFF

Airlines Clerk: You missed your plane?

Upset Passenger: Yes, I did.

Airlines Clerk: By how much did you miss it?

Upset Passenger: I missed it by one minute.

Airlines Clerk: Well, why are you so excited? The way you're carrying on, I thought you missed it by at least an hour!

First Woman: My son came to visit for his vacation.

Second Woman: Did you meet him at the airport?

First Woman: Goodness no. I've known him for years!

Woman: Can you give me a room and bath?

Hotel Clerk: I can give you a room, but you'll have to take your own bath!

Vacationer: What's the best way to prevent infection caused by biting insects?

Motel Owner: Don't bite any!

Fred: When my brother goes to the zoo, he needs two tickets.

Ted: Why?

Fred: One to get in and one to get out!

Matt: Did you know that camping attracts 50 million a year?

Noah: People or mosquitoes?

Paul: What made you nervous about the flight?

Robert: Seeing the pilot's instrument panel, and realizing it was in braille!

Father: We came all the way here on our vacation to see this parade. And now Mary is gonna miss it if she doesn't hurry. Where is she?

Daughter: She's upstairs, waving her hair.

Father: For Pete's sake, hasn't she got a flag??

A woman went shopping on vacation and asked the store clerk, "May I try on that dress in the window?"

"Well," replied the clerk, "don't you think it would be better to use the dressing room?"

Pete: You went to Alaska on your vacation? Was it cold up there?

Pat: You bet it was cold. It was so cold, the candles froze and we couldn't blow them out!

The man decided to try a new restaurant on his vacation, but it turned out to be a dive. "Waiter," he complained, "I don't like all these flies buzzing around my table."

"Yes, sir," replied the waiter. "You just point out to me the ones you don't like, and I'll chase them away!"

A young couple spent their vacation driving in the mountains. "Every time you race around one of those narrow curves," exclaimed the wife, "I just get terrified."

"Then do what I do," said her husband. "Close your eyes!"

Bill: I've never been to a dude ranch before. Is that horse you're riding well-behaved?

Ben: Sure is. He's got such good manners that when we come to a fence, he always stops and lets me go over first!

Vacationer: How much are these tomatoes?

Farmer: Two dollars a pound.

Vacationer: Two dollars? Did you raise them yourself?

Farmer: Sure did. They were only one dollar yesterday!

The vacationer paid his hotel bill, then yelled to the bellboy, "Please — hurry! Run up to room 1026 and see if I left my briefcase and overcoat. Hurry — please! I've got just six minutes to make my plane!"

Four minutes later, the bellboy came back, terribly out of breath. "Yes, sir," he reported. "They're up there!"

Why did the monster want to go surfing?

He wanted to hang eleven!

Where did the werewolf go on his vacation?

To the Baseball Howl of Fame.

Where is the vampire's favorite vacation spot?

Great Neck, New York.

What is the best thing about the witch's hotel?

Excellent broom service!

What is the werewolf's favorite hotel?

The Howl-iday Inn.

What is the ghosts' favorite beach?

Mali-boo!

Where do monsters travel?

From ghost to ghost!

Why was Dracula so unpopular at the vacation resort?

He was a pain in the neck!

What is the zombies' favorite vacation
resort?

Club Dead!

How did Dr. Frankenstein amuse his monster on vacation?

He kept him in stitches!

Why did the monster go to San Francisco?

He left his heart there.

What city is the witches' favorite vacation spot?

Witch-ita!

YOU KNOW IT'S GOING TO BE A ROTTEN VACATION WHEN . . .

. . . your mom didn't forget just your toothbrush this year — she forgot your whole suitcase!

. . . you have to share the backseat of the car with your nervous German shepherd, who insists on sitting on your lap the whole way!

IT'S GOING TO BE A ROTTEN VACATION WHEN . . .

. . . your sister gets carsick as you back down the driveway!

IT'S GOING TO BE A ROTTEN VACATION WHEN . . .

. . . your parents didn't realize that the camp they sent you to is a "speak-only-French" camp!

. . . no one can figure out why the water in the swimming pool turns your skin purple and green!

. . . even though you've already driven through 200 miles of farm country, your mother insists on pointing out every cow and horsie!

. . . the bird that chased you across the campsite turns out to be a mosquito!

IT'S GOING TO BE A ROTTEN VACATION WHEN...

... "Cozy Cabins" got its name because there's room inside for only one member of your family at a time!

(12)

WELCOME TO
COZY CABINS

IT'S GOING TO BE A ROTTEN VACATION WHEN . . .

. . . your parents believe you really love singing "Row, Row, Row Your Boat" as a round for mile after mile after mile.

. . . the manager of the campgrounds tells your dad that she makes most of her money from selling snakebite medicine!

LAST STOP FOR LAUGHS

Tim: Where did your mom go on vacation?
Jim: Alaska.
Tim: Never mind. I'll ask her myself!

Pam: Why are you doing the backstroke?
Sam: I just had lunch, and I don't want to swim on a full stomach!

"Is this Smith, Smith, Smith, and Smith?"

"Yes, it is, ma'am."

"Could I speak to Mr. Smith?"

"I'm sorry, but Mr. Smith is on vacation."

"Oh. May I speak to Mr. Smith then? It's very important."

"I'm so sorry, but Mr. Smith is also on vacation."

"Oh. Well, it's quite urgent. Let me speak to Mr. Smith then."

"Sorry. Mr. Smith is on vacation, too."

"I'm really desperate. Could I speak to Mr. Smith then?"

"Speaking!"

Max: Your girlfriend was sailing on vacation and fell overboard into shark-infested waters?

Mike: That's right. And the sharks didn't bother her.

Max: Why not?

Mike: They were *man*-eating sharks!

Gramps: I made two trips across the Atlantic and never took a bath!

Granny: I'd say that makes you a dirty double-crosser!

The family was on vacation, eating in a fancy restaurant, when the little boy complained, "Daddy, I don't like cheese with holes."

"Well, just eat the cheese and leave the holes on the side of your plate!"

While on vacation Tim and Jim went duck hunting with their hunting dogs. But they had no success. "I think I know the problem," said Tim. "I think I know what we're doing wrong."

"What, Tim?"

"We're not throwing the dogs high enough!"

Kim: Why did you miss the plane?

Jenny: I had to say good-bye to my pets.

Kim: But you're two hours late!

Jenny: I have an ant farm!

Susan: I don't think that photo you took of me on vacation does me justice.

Sharon: You don't want justice — you want mercy!

"I'm spending my vacation in the backyard. Like my new swimming pool?"

"It's great. But how come there's no water in it?"

"I can't swim!"

Max was enjoying his vacation until he was stopped on a dark street by a holdup man. "Stick 'em down!" cried the thief.

"Huh?"

"You heard me. Stick 'em down!"

"Don't you mean stick 'em up?" asked Max.

"Oh. No wonder I'm losing money at this!!"

"I'll have to give you a ticket, sir," said the traffic cop to the speeding vacationer. "You were doing 90 miles an hour."

"Nonsense," exclaimed the driver. "I've only been in the car for 10 minutes!"